God Pursues a Priest

God Pursues a Priest

George Rich

Regular Baptist Press
1300 North Meacham Road
Post Office Box 95500
Schaumburg, Illinois 60195

Cover design: Joe Ragont

Cover illustration: Joe VanSeveren

God Pursues a Priest
© 1986
Regular Baptist Press
Schaumburg, Illinois
Printed in U.S.A.

Library of Congress Cataloging-in-Publication Data

Rich, George, 1934–
  God pursues a priest.

  1. Rich, George, 1934–   . 2. Baptists—United States—
Clergy—Biography. 3. Episcopal Church—Controversial lit-
erature. 4. Anglican Communion—Controversial literature.
I. Title.
BX6495.R56A3 1986   248.2′4 [B]   86-10187
ISBN 0-87227-109-9

Contents

I fled Him, down the nights and down the days;
   I fled Him, down the arches of the years;
I fled Him down the labyrinthine ways
   Of my own mind; and in the mist of tears
I hid from Him. . . .

             Francis Thompson, "The Hound of Heaven"

Foreword

George Rich is certainly a unique and blessed token of God's grace. His conversion to Christ reminds us in some ways of the salvation experience of the great apostle Paul. Both men were very religious prior to their salvation and very committed to a system of teaching that promised liberation but that actually enslaved. It is so easy to be religious but lost—in complete ignorance of the basic concepts of salvation.

It was my privilege to work alongside George and his dedicated wife, Francoise, in the work of the gospel. It was plain to see that both of them had been marvelously changed by God's saving power. They had truly passed "from darkness into light."

Perhaps the most religious man in the annals of the Christian church wrote, "This is a faithful saying, and worthy of all acceptation, that Christ Jesus came into the world to save sinners; of whom I am chief" (1 Tim. 1:15). Do good people, even religious leaders, need personal salvation? Read one man's discovery of the answer.

ERNEST D. PICKERING, Th.D.

7

Introduction

Reading the manuscript of George Rich's book, I was reminded of the first time that he and his wife, Francoise, walked into Cedar Hill Baptist Church in Cleveland Heights, Ohio, where I was pastor. I could not then have imagined the dramatic events that preceded their visit that night. I saw them as an attractive young couple who were curious about our church. For some reason they wanted to see our baptistry. I knew nothing of their conversions or their desire to be baptized. Nor was there anything to indicate that Mr. Rich was an Episcopal priest. In time I would learn the details of an extraordinary story of God's pursuit of a man whose greatest need was the God he professed to represent but did not know.

Knowing that his life was empty and meaningless, Mr. Rich was confused and depressed. He could well have identified with Matthew Arnold's words in "Dover Beach" that this world

> Hath really neither joy, nor love, nor light,
> Nor certitude, nor peace, nor help for pain;
> And we are here as on a darkling plain
> Swept with confused alarms of struggle and flight,
> Where ignorant armies clash by night.

God found Mr. George Rich in his particular hiding place and brought him by grace beyond resistance to His saving embrace. You cannot read this story without seeing the glory of God in redemptive love and power and rejoicing in the runaway's capture and conversion.

JOHN BALYO, D.D.

# The Darkness Within

Chapter One

Fear had so overtaken me that I avoided every social contact I could. Dread and anxiety were my constant companions. Holding a coffee cup with just one hand, then placing it back on the saucer without anyone noticing the shaking, became one of my most terrifying challenges. Regular counseling with a qualified (that is, well-trained) minister and eventually with a psychiatrist, together with large doses of tranquilizers, brought no relief. I did not become tranquil; I became worse. My personal and private life was falling apart and my god, counseling with its arsenal of pills, was letting me down. Even alcoholic beverages, which had once brought temporary relaxation, had no positive effect. Sometimes excessive drinking only left me with a sense of failure, frequent morning-after headaches and a deeper sense of dread, despair and impending danger. Seldom was there relief from the fear, guilt and misery that dogged me daily.

From my present perspective, what made my life so tragic then was that I was an Episcopal priest. I was supposed to be a minister of God, a light shining out hope to a lost world. But God was not real to me, and there was no light within to shine without—no hope to be found in such an empty vessel. My existence was a pit of darkness with walls too steep to climb. Even a faithful wife and concerned friends were unable to lift me from my despair.

Now it must be clearly stated that what I am describing is symptomatic. The real cause of my misery was a life lived independently from God. His truth and instruction had no personal meaning or applicability to my life. He was nothing but a thought, an image that sometimes made me feel good, sometimes fearful. Any belief was totally intellectual, and it had no bearing on my life. My thoughts, my lusts and my desires were supreme. My idol of psychology had a certain power over my life, but it never commanded my total worship. Many idols and changing deities are the lot of those who fall short of genuine belief in the one true God. My gods frequently competed, each one receiving my devotion only as long as it could help me, a demanding and capricious rebel.

My shaking, fear and guilt, I now realize, were the result of total selfishness, or sin. They were the result of trying to live a life that was separate from and unrelated to the One Who alone could give true happiness and purpose to life.

One might fairly ask, "How could such a thing be? How could a minister fall into such unbelief and sin?" I will answer for myself and judge no one else.

There were psychological factors, I am sure, that led me into the ministry. The church seemed to offer a security that I needed. Some seek security in money, others seek it in power, success or health. I sought it in the church. I did not know that true security can only be found in God. As Augustine wrote in his *Confessions,* "For Thou madest us for Thyself, and our heart is restless, until it repose in Thee."

There was another reason, however, that I went into the ministry. From childhood I had had a problem with fear, not only of life but of death. I remember waking up terrified at a very young age and thinking about what would happen to me when I died. Would it be the end? This me that felt and enjoyed much of life, this mind that thought, this heart that could experience love and closeness—would it all be obliterated at death? When this body went into the grave, would all the personality and spirit and mind end with it? My thoughts would invariably conclude with picturing myself being lowered into the ground . . . the end. Fear would well up and I would sit up in bed with a terrible sense of vulnerability. I believed, shaking hands and all, that I could control most of my life, but this was beyond me. I knew that sooner or later I would die. It was totally uncontrollable and therefore unacceptable. So two influences converged and gave direction to my life and ultimately led to the ministry. The first was a desire to find God, or better yet, some hope of eternal life. The second was an intense desire to live life to the hilt, experiencing all I could, be it right or wrong. Only the fear of death and the possibility of eternal nothingness prevented greater excesses and sins. (I now recognize that this was the grace of God.) So sinful did my life become that I was surprised to discover God's preventing grace; yet it was there. At one point, I even determined to disavow God, having been influenced by the pathetic and wicked "God is dead" literature. Praise His name and loving grace, He would not let me "kill" Him. Oh, how great a God!

The third reason I went to seminary was because I was encouraged to do so by an Episcopal parish priest and by the bishop of that diocese.[1] I told these men that I believed in God and wanted to help people. I believed both statements to be true, and they were to a certain extent. I liked to think about God and argue about His existence in rap sessions at the University of Michigan. I believed that somehow there had to be a God. The grave just could not be the end, though I feared it might be. Still, this God was an idea and I could not let Him rule over *me*, my ultimate god of gods. I had never heard that I was personally responsible for my sin and that eternal life was mine if I would personally receive Jesus Christ as my Savior. In fact, I told a professor at the Episcopal seminary just before graduation and ordination that I did not see why it was necessary to believe in Christ as long as one believed in God. How great is the darkness of the nonbeliever.

My father was a successful lawyer. Through the years, although enjoying all of the benefits of a good income and a well-known father, I saw that materialism with all of its attendant pleasures and pressures was not really what life was all about. Therefore, my purpose in entering the ministry was to help people rather than to be successful materially. It was important to me to be a success as a person and to help others to be so. Little did I realize what great failure awaited me.

The Darkness Without

This chapter is about the Episcopal church. I am writing not in the spirit of bitterness but sadness. The Episcopal church, as well as many other mainline denominations, is enveloped in spiritual darkness. The light of Jesus Christ once shone in the Episcopal church, especially the Church of England. Cranmer, Latimer, Ridgely and others knew the truth and, I believe, the living God in a personal and real way. George Whitefield and John Wesley, two of the greatest preachers and lights of Christ in all the pages of church history, died without officially separating themselves from the Church of England. I do not believe that these men would remain in the Episcopal church today. A formal liturgy has replaced a living and vital faith in Christ among the people. No doubt there are exceptions; in fact, I know there are Episcopalians who have a personal faith in Christ, although I do not understand how their love for Him can allow them to remain involved in such compromise.

Yet, granting the fact of a few lights in the Episcopal church, the vast majority of its membership is in darkness. The Bible perfectly describes its worship, "Having a form of godliness, but denying the power thereof: from such turn away" (2 Tim. 3:5). You might ask, "How can you make such a claim about the Episcopal church? And if it is true, what is your motivation? Why publish such a statement?"

My basis for this claim is well founded. My grandfather, C. T. Rich, was an avid Episcopalian, as attested to by a beautiful stained glass window in an Episcopal church in Lakewood, Ohio. But his life, as far as I could tell, did not evidence an experience of God's saving grace. I hope my assessment is wrong. Only future judgments will tell.

My Presbyterian mother became an Episcopalian when she married my Episcopalian father. Like so many in this day, they were nominal Christians. Christmas, Easter and maybe another occasional Sunday during the year were the extent of church attendance. Other than an occasional "grace" at meals, which I usually offered (and that not until high school years), prayer was nonexistent. The Bible was never read or quoted or used as a directive.

Yet my sister Pat and I were duly christened and confirmed; the latter on the basis of being able to say the Lord's Prayer, the former on the basis of family custom. After all, we were Episcopalians. But, obviously, my baptism made no new impression on me and confirmation was personally meaningless.

Two other events stand out in my relationship to the church. The first is when I attended, for a Sunday, a Methodist church to be eligible for church league basketball. A determined teacher, group pressure and a desire to play basketball motivated me to sign a pledge never to drink or smoke. I signed it, but it was a burden. At this time, I do not recall that I either drank or smoked, but the restriction was bothersome to one who wanted to experience as much of life as possible.

The second experience was becoming an acolyte[1] in the Episcopal church. A friend wanted me to, the minister and the people were friendly, so I did. I liked the atmosphere, the beauty of the robes and appointments, the music, the experience of church. During this time, which also involved church basketball, I became acquainted with the associate rector. I asked him

about my oath to never drink or smoke. With all the authority
vested in him as a priest of the Episcopal church, he assured me
that I could do both with impunity and without guilt. That was
good news—just what I wanted to hear. In future debaucheries,
his statement often brought comfort. I do not blame him; I
believe the oath would have been broken with or without his
sanction. But the fact of his sanction does say something about
the mentality of the Episcopal church, and I do not think the
rector was a maverick. The widespread use of alcohol and smoking (the latter even in church buildings) among the members is
indicative of its worldly climate. The sin of the Episcopal
church is far more serious than these symptoms; the darkness is
far deeper and deadlier.

A libertine college career at the University of Michigan saw
only infrequent visits to the Episcopal church. I attended on
high holy days and when I felt guilty over excesses. Graduation
was upon me. A distaste for military service and an interest in
religion, plus an Episcopal curate who encouraged me to go to
seminary, combined to cause me to speak to my own rector and
bishop about the ministry.

A year of secular work and sinful pleasures interrupted my
seminary training. The schooling itself was a rather stilted experience. I felt that classes were boring, and worldliness was a way
of life among many of the students and some of the faculty.
Drinking, sometimes at a local pub, and smoking were common. God still was not personally real in my life, so I felt comfortable in this atmosphere, accepted by students and faculty
alike.

It was quite a different experience from my year of study,
years later, at a Baptist seminary where faculty and students
knew the Lord and sought to serve Him. The one experience
was godless, the other godly.

Upon my graduation from seminary, I became the curate of
a large suburban Episcopal church in Akron, Ohio. One of my
fellow graduates and ordinands told me I was going to an

ecclesiastic plum. This statement was from a worldly perspective, although I did not fully appreciate what a wealthy, sophisticated church it was until years later.

Before commenting on the religious life of that church, I want to say how much I appreciated the kindness of so many of the people. They were good to me and, after my marriage, to my wife as well. I considered the rector and fellow assistant to be friends and I still have concern for them. Now, as a Christian and teacher of God's Word, I believe their teaching to be mixed with grave error, as I will discuss in a later chapter. Because of the consistently erroneous teaching by this staff, myself included, and by previous ministers as well, the church was a far, far cry from New Testament Christianity. For most of the members, I am sure, it was a way of life—a very social life.

As an assistant in the large church, I began with others a "mission" church in a nearby community. A number of factors combined to make the work an almost instant success. Many of the members were wealthy and social, but although I still have affection toward them, I am not aware that there was any spiritual life in the congregation. No one ever witnessed to me about the need of accepting Jesus Christ—*personally*—as my Savior and Lord. And certainly, even as a minister, I was incapable of witnessing to anyone.

Because of an agreement with the rector of the larger church, once the mission church became organized with a membership of about fifty, I resigned and another was called to be the full-time minister. That was difficult, for I had been comfortable and happy and at home. But the Lord, unknown to me, had something better. So after a brief return to the large church, another church in Cleveland opened to me and my wife, Francoise, and we moved there—young, prideful, worldly and basically happy. As an assistant, I had been accepted, wined and dined in Akron; but now I was the minister and that brought conflict.

The conflict with members of this all white suburban

church, which had moved from the inner city as blacks moved into the area, was heightened by the volatile social conditions of the sixties. I was a liberal's liberal. Not long after my arrival at the church, we held a "unity service" with the black congregation from which the suburban church had departed. It went quite well, but it also created tension among some members of the church I served. The Vietnam War was also a focus of my ministry, and I participated in peace marches and other forms of protest. This was not appreciated by many of the church members. The pressure began to build. I began attending Group Dynamics and Sensitivity Training sessions,[2] which stripped away some of my defenses. Counseling sessions with a high, most respected Episcopal priest only encouraged me to accept myself, even in my increasingly apparent sinfulness.[3] My world was increasingly darkened by personal conflicts, a growing drinking problem and inability to sleep even when taking pills and drink to knock me out. The happy newlywed, with a nice suburban church, was facing the reality of sin in the church (hatred, power struggles, etc.) and sin within himself. I was miserable. To express the degree to which I sank is not necessary to the purpose of this book. Suffice it to say that I was a very sinful young man. When things were at their worst, vacation time came and my wife and I headed south to Florida. Loving, accepting parents and the balmy breezes did not bring the "healing" I had expected. I became worse. Much sin and a total breakdown characterized our two-month vacation. The church graciously granted me extra vacation time.

I cannot overemphasize that the Episcopal church is in darkness. In the sixties, while I was there, none of the leading clergy ever witnessed to me a Biblical testimony of saving faith in Christ, even in the most intimate counseling sessions. Cataloging my sins never brought rebuke or an invitation to Jesus Christ for forgiveness and power over sin. Never in the almost eleven years that I served in this church did I hear a gospel message exhorting sinners to be saved. (See Appendix B, p. 53, for a sample of a typical sermon I preached during those years). At this writing it has been over fifteen years since I left the Episcopal church. Many will say that it has all changed since then. I do not think so, for reasons that will be given in a later chapter.

My return from Florida found me no better. In fact, I was worse than when I had left. Survival was my main goal—just making it without total collapse. I do not think the church recognized what a difficult time I was having.

One day I asked the janitor, Clarence Radcliffe, if he had heard anything about my problems. He said no, and asked me two questions in the course of our conversation. First, did I know for certain that God had ever answered a prayer? Second, did I know what would happen to me when I died? I went home after our conversation and found myself seriously contemplating these two questions. I remembered once during a Lenten meeting telling a number of people that God had answered a prayer. But now as I considered Clarence's first question, I could not say that I knew for sure that God had answered the prayer or if it was just a coincidence. Now I realize that Clarence was helping me to see that I had no faith. It astounds me that I had been an ordained minister for eight-and-a-half years and was not sure if God had answered one prayer. How happy I am to know today that it is God Who answers great and small prayers, and that there is no coincidence in the life of a child of God.

Next I considered Clarence's second question. You may recall that I have said that one of my great fears was that of dying.

It held me in bondage. The Bible has a verse that perfectly describes my former condition, "And deliver them *who through fear of death were all their lifetime subject to bondage"* (Heb. 2:15). So, afraid of dying, I was unable to live. Therefore, I sinned in what I thought to be "safe" ways, although many were not. I thank God that He in His love and grace kept me from dying, a sinner who had so offended His holiness, until I trusted Jesus Christ as my Savior and Lord.

What would happen to me when I died? The same terror that had gripped me as a child would grip me now with equal force any time I let myself ponder death. I knew it was the great question. What is next? Where do I go? Is death the end? As long as I was alive, there was hope of finding peace about this fearful unknown. Although struggling personally, there were still moments of happiness and affection. There was existence, and who could honestly think of it just ending. I really believe that the reason for much of my drinking and other sinful activity was to forget this terrifying prospect. So successful was I that on numerous occasions I foolishly risked my life—jumping freights, hanging from a bridge of enormous height by one hand and many other dangerous actions.

Somewhere during this time I remember seeing the view back to earth from one of the space shots. How beautiful—all white and blue; but around it was utter blackness, a void of darkness, nothingness. It reminded me of what I would one day be, as far as I knew. I felt that the camera was taking my picture. I was on that beautiful ball, in Ohio, and I was alive; but one day I would die. Then my existence would be like that outer darkness, that void, that nothingness. I felt this more than understood it; it was a condition described well by many of the existentialists, men who could accurately diagnose the dreadful human condition without God but who had no cure to offer.

Realizing that I did not know for sure that even one of my prayers had ever been answered and that I certainly did not know what would happen upon death, I talked with Clarence again and asked if he knew what would happen to him when he died. Was it really possible for one to know? Yes, Clarence knew, and I believed him. Could I know? Yes, this dear, genuine Christian man assured me that I too could know.

What was to follow cannot be put in any orderly sequence, but there are very special events that happened which should be noted.

First, on an occasion or two, Clarence and I prayed that I might be saved. I was sincere, but I was not saved at those times. Clarence did not say something like, "Now you are saved. You asked; God has to save you because He keeps His promise. It's the devil making you doubt, if you do." I was not saved, but not because God is not faithful to His Word. He heard me and loved me, but I was without faith. I did not really believe at that time that Jesus Christ saved me when I called. God knew He would save me in His time. The faith would come by God's grace and in His perfect will.

The matter of faith then became the great question of my life. If I could get it, I could be saved. I wanted, I willed to be saved.

Something that I can only accept as the grace of God happened in my life at that time. The Bible, which had literally meant no more to me than any other book, became to me what it in fact is—namely, the Word of God. It became the authority of my life. I knew for the first time that it is true, it is infallible, it tells us what we are to know of God and of ourselves. Before this miracle of God's grace, the Bible had been no more important to me than a newspaper article, a novel by Jean-Paul Sartre, a theology book by Paul Tillich or (and especially) my own thoughts. Now it became the absolute standard!

Two portions of Scripture spoke to me as I began to read the Bible. Clarence had told me to read the Bible and pray *only* for my salvation, kindly stating that my prayers for others would not do any good anyway. I had to be saved first. I read in Romans 8:1, "There is therefore now no condemnation to them which are in Christ Jesus, who walk not after the flesh, but after the Spirit."

Never before had the Bible spoken to me personally. The word *now* really stood out. Paul was writing that there had been a time when he was condemned. With my liberal theological training, and the Word of God not being the authority in my life until this time, I had believed about whatever suited me. I do not think that I believed in a literal hell; so condemnation had meant only something bad, something that I wanted to avoid, something like annihilation or nonexistence. Now, although it was still a considerable length of time before I came to faith in Jesus Christ, it can certainly be said that God was working in my life. For the first time, I realized that I personally might have a problem with God. I came to see that He was holy and I was sinful and that was why I was under His condemnation. I saw myself, not society or my environment, as personally responsible to God for my sin.

I thought of my baptism as an infant, my confirmation and even ordination, realizing that none of those events were the *now* that could bring me out of my condemnation. That is about as far as this verse went for me at that time.

The other verse that spoke to me was Romans 8:28, "And we know that all things work together for good to them that love God, to them who are the called according to his purpose." This verse assured me that Jesus Christ could put my life together, when I believed it to be ruined and practically over. He could also work all that had happened to a good purpose. I took comfort in this.

Clarence and I continued to meet and talk about the Bible. He was very faithful; he would take the time to answer any questions that I had, sometimes shortchanging himself on sleep, I am sure. Although I do not recall specific verses or the exact content of these discussions, no doubt they were all important in leading to my conversion to Christ.

One day at the church, two fundamental Baptist ministers

stopped by to see if they could borrow the church building to hold revival meetings. As I recall, I asked them how they knew whether or not members in their church were saved. That, I now perceive, was like throwing ground round to a hungry dog. The next thing I knew, they were in my office talking from God's Word and praying. These men took me to Romans 10:17, ". . . Faith cometh by hearing, and hearing by the word of God."

I remember thinking, "You read the Word and just believe it; that's faith." Perhaps I really did believe it at that point, but I was not assured. I was afraid it was not personal and real. It may be that I wanted an experience, something unusual, a sign—something I could see or rest on for assurance. I was probably looking inward to see if I had faith rather than outward to Christ, trusting Him to save me, simply believing His Word. I shared my lack of assurance with Clarence. He encouraged me to keep reading the Scripture and to keep praying for my salvation. It was easy for me to read the Bible. I could understand it and it was personal, and yet I still could not find peace regarding my personal salvation. Within a week Clarence and I met again, on a Tuesday, in the church building. Clarence led me to pray after him a prayer that called out to Jesus Christ for forgiveness. I believe that in that moment I was saved. A burden lifted and the fear of death was gone. I believe the Holy Spirit indwelt me at that time. Driving home to tell my wife, who had been saved three weeks before, I remember thinking that if the little VW was totalled in an accident and I died, I would go to Heaven. That was the faith for which I had been searching—a gift from God. My wife was so happy for me, and a born-again church member said to me that night when she saw me, "You have been saved." Praise the Lord.

What happened to me was experiential, but I believe it was spiritual and not just emotional. That first faith was ever so weak, although I believe it was God-given. However, I want to be painfully honest to be of help to others. There was a long battle with assurance. I see this as a matter of temperament. At the same time, I can write today that I know I am saved because my faith is in Jesus Christ Who has promised to save those that call upon Him. Many verses put my fears to rest:

> Fear not: for I have redeemed thee, I have called thee by thy name; thou art mine (to apply a promise to Israel and to me) (Isa. 43:1b). All that the Father giveth me shall come to me; and him that cometh to me I will in no wise cast out (John 6:37). For whosoever shall call upon the name of the Lord shall be saved (Rom. 10:13).

My security and hope is in Jesus Christ alone, in His shed blood for me. Romans 4:23–25 says, "Now it was not written for his sake alone, that it was imputed to him; But for us also, to whom it shall be imputed, if we believe on him that raised up Jesus our Lord from the dead; *Who was delivered for our offences, and was raised again for our justification.*" God has given me these verses and I rest my eternity securely on His Word, His promise, His faithfulness to me, a sinner for whom Christ died, a one-time enemy of Jesus Christ, an unknowing pawn of Satan and sin. So often I have been comforted by the following verses, as if God had Paul write them for me personally:

> *And I thank Christ Jesus our Lord, who hath enabled me, for that he counted me faithful, putting me into the ministry: Who was before a blasphemer, and a persecutor, and injurious: but I obtained mercy, because I did it ignorantly in unbelief.* And the grace of our Lord was exceeding abundant with faith and love which is in Christ Jesus. This is a faithful saying, and worthy of all acceptation, that Christ Jesus came into the world to save sinners; of whom I am chief. Howbeit for this cause I obtained mercy, that in me first Jesus Christ might shew forth all longsuffering, for a pattern to them which should hereafter believe on him to life everlasting. Now unto the King eternal, immortal, invisible, the only wise God, be honour and glory for ever and ever. Amen (1 Tim. 1:12–17).

What joy filled my soul upon my salvation. I remember getting up in the morning rested, at peace and with a purpose in life. Before my conversion, I had thrown away all my pills and had given up smoking and drinking. I had cried out to God after a night of sin, "Jesus, if you exist, I somehow believe you will save me. If not, it will not make any difference what happens to me anyway." He heard that prayer, that cry of total despair—it had been my lowest point in life.

But all that was past. The sun, the trees, the gentle breezes took on a beauty and fullness that I had never perceived before. What a glorious, loving God Who made this beautiful world and me; Who redeemed me; Who forgave me; Who gave me life—real life—with meaning and purpose. My only purpose now was to please Him in all that I did. I believed myself to be His special possession—His child and servant. How free I felt, free to serve and worship. What love for others I experienced, especially sinners. How sorry I felt for them and how much I desired to win them to a saving knowledge of Christ. I am happy to say, too, that God has increased my faith through prayerful reading of His Word to the place of complete assurance.

Notwithstanding what has just been stated, one day I felt quite discouraged. I recall that it was the Friday or Saturday after the Tuesday of my salvation. Clarence was at the church and we talked. Thank God for faithful, selfless servants and brothers in Christ. He suggested that I needed to tell my church about my salvation and give an invitation. It was too much to consider and I dismissed the suggestion immediately. I found it impossible, however, to prepare a message for Sunday. No matter how much I tried, I couldn't. Unknown to me, God was working His perfect will. Kneeling as the hymn before the sermon dwindled away, I was at a loss, and yet I knew what I was to do. For the first time in my life, I simply told my story, from childhood. I told about it for a long time, much longer than a sermon would have been. After telling of my conversion, I gave an invitation—not really knowing anything about it, except to say, "If you want to accept Christ, please come forward to the altar rail." Now things like this just do not happen in the Episcopal church—at least, they did not then in any church I knew. To my amazement, three came forward wanting to be forgiven and saved, calling upon the name of Jesus Christ. Several were saved during the next three weeks, and Christmas had never been so full and real. I remember singing a familiar hymn and seeing for the first time, "He came to give us *second birth.*" Thank You, Lord, for the eyes to see. Little did I know that my salvation would completely change the direction of my life.

The Break

As I said, several persons received Christ as Savior at the Episcopal church. It was a thrilling time filled with blessings and challenges. But it was time for me to leave. A number of factors combined to cause me to leave the Episcopal church, even though it was the church of my youth and the place of my security. In my wife's testimony, she has frequently noted that we knew nothing else; our lives had been tied up with the Episcopal church. Although numerous factors converged in making such a momentous decision, I believe the major dynamic was doctrinal. In fact, over the years, in my mind I had been periodically resigning; but I never really could because of the security the church offered. Now, for the first time, I had a message to preach and a sense of knowing what I was about as a person and a minister. Christ was with me and whatever I would do would be all right just as long as I was in His will. It is important to understand that I was enjoying preaching and the increase in attendance and giving because some other born-again Episcopalians began attending services. They encouraged me not to leave but to establish a Bible-based, gospel-preaching Episcopal church. Still, I was troubled for several reasons, all of which reduce finally to matters of doctrine.

First, upon realizing that I was not saved, and with the advice of Clarence, I had told the bishop of the diocese of my

29

unregenerate condition. Had he told me to resign, I would have. Had he led me to Christ, or at least attempted to, I would have had more difficulty leaving the Episcopal church. What he told me was astounding. He said that as far as he knew, none of the 120 priests in his diocese had had that one-time experience with God that some groups (churches) talk about. Then he said, in effect, "As for me, I have had many experiences with God, and not just this one experience which you seek. Don't worry about it. I'm glad for your life and ministry."

Later, after my salvation, I made another appointment with the bishop and told him that I had been saved. He said he was impressed because I had told him before that I believed I would be saved and now I was. In a very friendly manner he invited me to tell him my story. I explained how the Bible taught that each must be born again to be saved, and that it was not a process but occurred in a moment of time upon trusting Jesus Christ for salvation. A process of conviction and searching might lead to that moment, but salvation was a free gift received by faith instantaneously.

It was then necessary to explain that there were three prerequisites for my continuing as a minister in the Episcopal church. The first was that I would give an invitation at the end of each service so that convinced people might come forward to be dealt with about their personal salvation. So far, so good. He agreed. Second, it would be necessary to baptize converts by immersion. He said that this would be no problem, other than finding a suitable place, since Episcopal churches do not have baptistries. The Book of Common Prayer allows by rubric either sprinkling or immersion. Third, I expressed my intention to be baptized personally by immersion, since Scripture teaches the necessity of salvation prior to baptism; and further, that the Bible teaches total immersion as the only mode of baptism. At this the bishop was very displeased, stating he would defrock me unless I reconsidered and that a letter would be forthcoming to that effect. As I recall, I tried to tell him kindly that it really made no differ-

ence since I would be separating from the Episcopal church anyway. Eventually the letter did come after I had sent him a copy
of my resignation. He did not defrock me but suspended me. My
letter of resignation was written January 17, 1971 and his letter
on January 22, 1971. His letter was warm and friendly, as was a
subsequent letter regarding our respective views of salvation and
water baptism. I appreciated his kindness very much and still
do, but his views were quite unscriptural. The letter on baptism
I do not believe I have a right to publish as it is personal to me,
nor do I believe it would be ethical to print excerpts, lest I be ac-
cused of editorializing. Besides, the issue of my leaving the Episcopal church did not center on the bishop's erroneous understanding of Biblical baptism but rather on the doctrine of the
church as found in the Book of Common Prayer. Since the
letter regarding my suspension was public, being sent in trip-
licate,[1] I will quote it in full as it will shed light on the contro-
versy. (See Appendix A, p. 51.) I have a genuine love for this
bishop and many other of my Episcopal associates. Perhaps I
should have done more to maintain a relationship, but to do so
is difficult when there is a difference regarding basic spiritual
issues. "Can two walk together, except they be agreed?"

While this exchange with the bishop was going on, other
events were rapidly taking place. For one, Clarence and I were
studying the Book of Common Prayer and comparing it with
the Bible. Three problems confronted us.

The first had to do with "The Office of the Burial of the
Dead." Because the office assumes that all that are buried from
the Episcopal church are true Christians, the service is misleading. An unsaved person might assume that he will go to Heaven
because no emphasis is made regarding the difference between
the saved and the lost. To illustrate, one of the prayers in the
Burial Office states, ". . . and grant that, increasing in knowledge and love of thee, he may go from strength to strength, in
the life of perfect service, in thy heavenly kingdom; through
Jesus Christ our Lord. . . ." I understand that the entire service

is in the name of Jesus Christ; but without a clear preaching of the gospel, it tends to make people think that all who are buried from the church are saved. I am reasonably sure that many buried through this office have had no personal knowledge of Jesus Christ and therefore have not gone from "strength to strength, in the life of perfect service " but rather have gone to hell. May the Lord have mercy on all those who, knowingly or unknowingly, jeopardize souls through this religious ritual. The Office of the Burial of the Dead has much to commend it but only as applied to true believers. It is no longer valid, indeed, it is misleading in a church with an unregenerate membership.

The second problem was with "The Office of Holy Communion." Without discussing the doctrinal questions of the real presence of Christ, I am concerned that the service is again misleading. Again, no distinction is made between the saved and the unsaved. So, at best, a mixed assembly participates in the Eucharist. People in all kinds of spiritual conditions assume that God's grace is received through the elements, whether or not real faith is present. Theologians may argue the doctrinal implications of Holy Communion, but the people think their participation makes them acceptable to God, even without a personal faith in Jesus Christ. I know personally a number of people who were once in this condition.

The third and greatest problem I have with the Book of Common Prayer centers on "The Ministration of Holy Baptism." The problems mentioned with burial and communion are really only an extension of the error of infant baptism. The Prayer Book states, after the child is sprinkled, "Seeing now, dearly beloved brethren, that this child is regenerate, and grafted into the body of Christ's church. . . ." This means a child is saved (regenerate) and made a member of Christ's spiritual body by this rite. The Bible states, "For ye are all the children of God *by faith* in Christ Jesus" (Gal. 3:26). By faith, not sprinkling, one is saved. The Bible teaches this again and again. We are saved, we are regenerate, we are born again by a personal faith in Jesus Christ and not by a rite or ceremony of the church.

> For therein is the righteousness of God revealed from faith to
> faith: as it is written, The just shall live by faith (Rom. 1:17).
> To declare, I say, at this time his righteousness: that he might be
> just, and the justifier of him which believeth in Jesus (Rom.
> 3:26). Therefore being justified by faith, we have peace with God
> through our Lord Jesus Christ (Rom. 5:1).

This doctrine of infant baptism will lead many sinners to hell. It invites, it necessitates an unregenerate church membership. It makes the unenlightened assume that they are Christians by virtue of their baptism. This leads to confusion in communion and burial and makes confirmation an inconsistency. The whole system is unbiblical and misleading. For these reasons I could not, in good conscience, remain in the Episcopal church, for it would have meant compromise and endorsing the teaching of error.

Also, during this time of decision, the Lord brought to me a number of Scriptural passages that convinced me He was leading me out of the Episcopal church.

Conversations with Episcopal priests who were professing believers and with others who were not, and conversations with some Baptist ministers were among other factors that caused me to leave.

Leaving was, and still is, a sadness. The Episcopal church was my heritage. It offered much security. But I could no longer embrace its doctrine and what I judged to be unbelief in the rank and file, as well as in the leadership,[2] of the Episcopal church. I saw no evidence of people with a genuine, personal faith in Jesus Christ.

We left the Episcopal church, quite literally, on January 20, 1971, submitting a written resignation to a church officer and then verbally resigning at the annual meeting. I stayed for about two weeks to conclude counseling and administrative matters. I did not conduct services for several reasons, the main one being that I would have had to compromise. For instance, the communion service was celebrated weekly, and my views have already been expressed regarding this service.

On the evening of January 20, 1971, my wife and I attended the Cedar Hill Baptist Church in Cleveland. Our new life in Christ, begun at the time of our conversion, would now start to take form.

First Steps in the New Life

"**What will we** do?" asked Francoise, as we returned home after resigning from the Episcopal church. My dear wife was concerned about our future. She had given up her native country of France to marry me; she had been quickly "converted" into an Episcopalian (it would not have worked to have had a Roman Catholic wife); she had now left, with her husband, all her worldly security upon resigning. I said that we had to begin our new life and that it was important to go that same night to a fundamental church. But which one? Clarence had mentioned Dr. John Balyo at Cedar Hill Baptist Church. Clarence's mother, a Christian and an invalid, had heard Dr. Balyo over the radio. Clarence said he was sure we would find a sound message and real Christians at that church. We took out the newspaper church page and began to look for the time of the evening service. I knew where the church was because it had been pointed out to me as a racist church which was growing because of its stand. How untrue that statement was, made by jealous, misguided liberals, I believe. The church was about twenty miles from where we lived and we were hesitant about driving that distance. We were also somewhat anxious about attending a Baptist church. We didn't know what to do, so we prayed and asked God to direct us to the church we should attend. Then we drove, ending up at Cedar Hill Baptist Church, thinking we had found a special event because of the full parking lot on a Sunday night. (Most Episcopal churches do not have Sunday night services.) As we walked toward the building, I asked God to help me feel comfortable—which I thought would be impossible without His aid—if it were the church for us. I walked into the sanctuary and was at home.

There are several observations that must be noted at this point. They will be instructive, I trust, regarding the difference between the liberal and fundamental church. These are general remarks since each local church has its own makeup.

First, I was struck with the atmosphere at Cedar Hill. It was friendly and reverent at the same time. Somehow I had expected an emotionalism; instead, we found a pleasant, worshipful surrounding. Three or four men took the chairs on the platform in regular suit clothes, which I liked. I was accustomed to vestments and clerical attire. When Dr. Balyo began to preach, my heart leaped for joy. He was articulate, intelligent and easy to hear. Most of all, I heard the truth and rejoiced in its simplicity. He preached on the parable of the wicked vineyardmen, the blind, misguided Pharisees. What a blessing it was to understand the Bible, for until my salvation I had not been able to make sense of it. It was so clear and it spoke not so much to my head as to my heart. I also recognized myself in the Pharisees and rejoiced that God had saved me out of darkness and confusion, forgiving my sins of ignorance and unbelief and leading me to the light, to faith and understanding. I left the service rejoicing. The only negative response concerned the music. I missed the more formal classical music and the hymns that were more familiar. Before long this changed, however, as I grew to love the hymns that are really love songs to Christ, warm and personal. The entire service was real and personal and alive, far different from what I had left.

Second, the people were authentically friendly. They seemed interested, really interested in us. They showed us the baptistry, which I requested to see because of my desire to be

baptized. We felt close to the people we met almost immediately. There were none of the more social courtesies which we
so easily would have recognized. There was genuineness and
love, which I now recognize as the Spirit of Christ.

This interest in us continued, and still does, through the
years. Some of those dear friends still pray for us. When we
showed up at the midweek service, the pastor and others were
delighted. We had not filled out a visitor's card, and they
thought we were gone for good. We recall all of those first con-
tacts with the highest thankfulness and real joy.

Third, things at Cedar Hill Baptist Church and subsequent
fundamental churches made sense. Baptism followed salvation.
I recognized that as Biblical. The Lord's Supper was a memori-
al, not complicated with a ritual and theology that few really
understood. There is a sense in the fundamental church of people understanding and participating in the communion and all
services. The Episcopal church was cold and ritualistic, even
austere by comparison. I truly believe that the main reason for
the difference is the blessing of God upon the one and not the
other. The Holy Spirit was present in the worship at Cedar Hill
Baptist Church in a way that He was not, I believe, in the Episcopal church. Where the Spirit of the Lord is there is liberty;
there is good sense and simplicity. I remember thinking in those
early days, This is the way it should be.

Fourth, there was a difference in the way one became a
member. In the liberal church, members were allowed to join if
they wanted to join. Maybe something had to be agreed to or
memorized, like the Lord's Prayer or Apostles' Creed, but most-
ly the motivation was, "Get the new member." Frequently, new
people taught or led right away because willing helpers were
needed. There was little concern about doctrine or belief. No
one was ever asked if he was saved. In fact, I know of no Episcopal church where that was asked. If one was asked if he believed
in Jesus Christ, the question meant, Do you believe He lived,
died and rose again? The question was directed to the intellect,

not to the heart, the seat of true Biblical belief.

In contrast, membership in the Baptist church, at least in Cedar Hill and churches of its fellowship, is quite a different matter. My wife and I gave our testimonies of salvation four times officially and several other times unofficially before being baptized and admitted to membership. We gave our testimonies in the New Members Class, before the deacon board, at our baptism and at a Wednesday night service when we were officially *voted* in as members. Why so many times? The people cared enough to be careful that we really understood salvation. They also wanted the blessing of hearing once again how the grace of God had drawn a lost sinner to Himself by faith in Jesus Christ. There was concern for the purity of the church too. Any Biblical church seeks to have only a regenerate membership.

It is difficult to imagine two more opposite motivations and approaches to church membership. The difference is literally like that between night and day. This is another reason why I left the Episcopal church. I believe these liberal churches that have no real membership requirements have a predominantly unregenerate membership. The leaders, and I was one, do not understand salvation. I do not think it is possible to reclaim these churches, only to witness to individuals, hoping that they will believe in Christ personally for their salvation and then separate to a true, Biblical church. I believe 2 Corinthians 6:14-17 describes the situation perfectly. The liberal church is made up of lost people. When they accept Christ, they need to separate from that system of darkness to a true Biblical church. The Bible, the Word of God, is light, and it is fundamental and not liberal churches that teach and believe it.

Fifth, I want to mention the matter of authority. I realize that this section as well as some others I have written are somewhat sketchy, but the purpose of this book is not to present a scholarly defense of fundamentalism. The purpose is to give an overview of one person's experience with Christianity today. What is to be the authority in one's life? This is very important.

The Episcopal church cites the Bible as the final authority, but it also allows secondary authorities such as church councils and traditions (the Thirty-nine Articles of Religion, VI, XX, XXI, XXXIV). Practically speaking, the Word of God is secondary, not being understood by an unregenerate membership. Tradition and decrees by the House of Bishops determine the doctrine and practice of the church. Decisions of men direct the church, and these decisions do not always correspond with the Word of God. One example would be the fiasco regarding the late Bishop Pike's rejection of the Virgin Birth. He was not reprimanded by the House of Bishops. It was simply stated that he did not speak for the whole church. Politically motivated compromise was the basis of the decision. Practice is removed from what the Thirty-nine Articles teach.[1] Frankly, the architects of those Articles and the Book of Common Prayer would hardly recognize the Episcopal church today. They would be sick at heart; I believe they would leave either by their own choice or the church's.

By way of conclusion, I want to list a few other differences between the Episcopal church and the Baptist church.

Most Baptist churches actively call and evangelize. Liberal churches do not, at least not with the gospel; they may invite someone to church. In the Baptist church, adults study the Bible in Sunday School and many on Wednesday, in addition to Sunday morning and evening services—four hours compared to one in the Episcopal church. Baptist churches recognize man's sinfulness; liberal churches try to fan a flame of goodness that the natural man simply does not possess (Rom. 3:10–12). Baptist preachers preach the truth and run the risk of offending some, and most sound Baptist churches want that kind of a preacher. Liberals want the kind of preacher that will make them feel good and scratch itching ears (2 Tim. 4:3). On and on I could go in listing great and significant differences.

To the degree that the Episcopal church I know represents mainline churches, I can say without reservation that believers have no right staying within that apostate system. There may be some sound individual churches, but by and large I am convinced that there is no gospel, no Spirit and no salvation. Liberalism, like Egypt of the Old Testament, has an appeal to the flesh, but it offers nothing but spiritual destruction.

I have never regretted leaving the Episcopal church and going to that first Sunday night service at Cedar Hill Baptist Church, even though I left my heritage and worldly security behind.

Because I am a Christian and because I believe the Bible, I am a fundamentalist. What I once looked down upon I am now pleased to be, for it means that God has been gracious to me.

The Faithful God

How precious to the believer is the truth, "Faithful is he that calleth you, who also will do it" (1 Thess. 5:24). God saved my wife and me in His perfect will and time. He has taught us, but more than that, He has directed our path, He has ordered our way, even step by step. He saved us from hell and He saved us for a purpose and it has been a blessing to see that purpose unfold. With all our failures, weaknesses and sins, He has blessed us and used us to introduce others to His gospel.

After separating from the Episcopal church and joining Cedar Hill Baptist Church, the basic spiritual question was resolved for us. What was not resolved was what to do with our lives. Without the Lord I would have been frantic, an emotional wreck. I know I would have tried to escape the pressures by drink and pills. Although without employment for a number of months, we had peace and enjoyed the blessing of the Lord. We knew we were saved children of God and we used much of this time to grow in the Word and to witness to friends, relatives, anyone we could. It was during this time that I had the privilege of leading my mother to Christ and my wife, Francoise, led my sister to Christ. Both my mother and sister are growing in the Lord. We have seen professions of faith in the last twelve years by two nieces and their husbands, one of whom I led to Christ. We have led two elderly aunts to Christ also. Some of our relatives are not at all happy with what has happened in our lives and we have experienced some direct opposition, but that has lessened somewhat. We rejoice in the grace and the power of God when we recall how some of these who now love Christ were at one time so opposed to His gospel. My father is noteworthy. At one time he was extremely hostile to the truth of salvation by faith in Jesus Christ. He is now, by God's grace, a professing Christian. How powerful and gracious God is. "Faithful is he that calleth you, who also will do it."

I might also note that during this time of unemployment and perhaps even sometime after obtaining work, my wife and I had the privilege of seeing some Episcopalians from our former church accept the Lord as Savior.

It was during this time, too, that God sent us our son Matthew by adoption. We decided to witness to the Episcopalian social worker as to why I was unemployed. We had learned that the gospel could quickly offend people. We prayed for God's help and blessing, that a witness to her would not jeopardize the adoption. God again was faithful. Although the social worker did not receive Christ, she not only did nothing to prevent the adoption but went out of her way to be helpful. I am not at liberty to fully express how kind she was to us, especially considering that the adoption was completed during the time of my unemployment. We saw this as God's faithfulness to us; we believe He blessed us because we endeavored to put Him first.

After pounding the pavements of Cleveland, passing out numerous resumes, following employment leads given by Christian friends, a job finally presented itself. It was a position as secretary of the Cleveland City Club, at a salary far greater than I had ever made before. I believe I would have enjoyed it, for it would have involved me in the political arena which I found exciting and interesting. But while I was grateful to those who offered the job, after much prayer I turned it down because my job description included ordering alcoholic beverages for the bar. I would not have served drinks but simply signed checks.

However, my new church had a covenant that stated that we would not be involved with anything having to do with the use or sale of alcohol as a beverage. All of my life I had compromised what few convictions I had. I was not going to do that now that I had accepted Christ. I wanted to please Him and be faithful. I was grateful to Him for saving me and I felt tremendous loyalty to my fellowship of believers. By God's grace I have sought to live by my convictions from that time on, whatever the cost. To whatever degree I have succeeded, it is all to God's glory and to the praise of His grace. There is no doubt in my mind what I would have done about that job prior to my conversion.

At that time of saying no to the offer of the City Club job, I had been unemployed for about six months. It is embarrassing to write, but I could not find a job; I was even turned down as a taxicab driver.

Employment finally came to me through an unusual set of circumstances. We attended a graduation party and met the administrator of a private boys' school in Cleveland, who was looking for an English teacher. Although I told him that I had no teaching degree, he hired me and obtained a special certification from the State of Ohio on the basis of my academic degrees. Although I tried never to use my lectures as a pulpit, the boys soon knew that I was a Christian and that I believed in God and in absolutes. Another faculty member was also a Christian and the Lord used us to see five boys profess Christ as Savior. When contracts for the new academic year were issued, we each received one. Mine had a substantial salary increase and I was praying about the Lord's will as to whether I should stay at the school. During that time, the Lord opened up an opportunity to witness to about ten to fifteen boys sitting in a hallway after school. As I walked out of my office, I overheard them talking about Christ. Soon I was part of the conversation, which lasted fifteen or twenty minutes. There was a rabbi's son and some other Jewish boys. A few days later I was called into the administrator's office and encouraged to sign the contract, but now with the understanding that I would not talk of Christ at all from eight to five. Believing that I had never used school time inappropriately to be a witness, which the school administrator agreed with, I decided not to sign the contract. He admitted that he was under some pressure from the board. He also acknowledged that our witness was true, but he was not ready to accept Christ personally, for he would not sacrifice his life-style in order to be saved. I was not happy at the school; it was too limiting in terms of possibility for witness and I felt insufficiently qualified for some of my responsibilities. I left on a friendly basis with the school authorities and I now see God's faithfulness in leading me there for the year. I believe there was some fruit and I grew much as a Christian.

Let me relate the story of one of the boys. When Ed's parents enrolled him at the school, school officials gave my name as a possible ride to school. When Ed looked up my name in the phone book, he saw the designation *Rev.* He asked why I, an ordained minister, was in school work. God had prepared Ed. He took my suggestion to read the Bible and he soon was saved. After my fellow Christian teacher and I left the school, Ed continued to witness to faculty and students alike. How faithful God is.

The next five years were spent at the Baptist Christian School of Cleveland, Ohio, primarily in the capacity of Bible teacher. One of these years was spent at the Grand Rapids Baptist Seminary, where I was granted an M.R.E. degree.

From there I went to be the principal of a Christian day school in Englewood, Florida. After that, I was led of God to First Baptist Church in Bremen, Indiana. After nearly three years of ministry as the pastor of that church, God has led us to Emmanuel Baptist Church in Toledo, Ohio, to serve as the assistant to the pastor in the area of evangelism. Although the senior pastor, Dr. Ernest Pickering, has recently been called of God to a new position, I thank God for the nearly two years I worked with him. I have grown tremendously in Christ through observing his godly walk and through his incomparable preaching of the Scriptures. I truly thank God for the privilege of serving as his assistant. He and his wife, Yvonne, have been used of God greatly in the lives of Francoise and me.

At the time of this writing, we have been at Emmanuel Baptist Church for over two years. Truly "the lines are fallen unto me in pleasant places; yea, I have a goodly heritage." We rejoice in our labors and have experienced God's blessings in our lives and ministries. "Faithful is he that calleth you, who also will do it."

Postscript

Dear reader, may I take this opportunity to ask you the same questions that Clarence asked me? Do you know for certain that you have eternal life and would go to Heaven should you die this day? Do you know for certain that God has answered your prayers, especially that most important one about your personal salvation by faith in Jesus Christ?

Some fifteen years ago I was religious but lost. Sometimes people say to me, "How could you have preached and not have been saved?" I answer that when we are in darkness we only have a head knowledge, not a heart knowledge, of the truth. I believe that many ministers like myself, however sincere they may be, are lost in liberalism. Many lay people are in the same condition, being led by blind leaders that cannot tell them how to be saved because they do not know themselves. Countless people will perish within Christendom, believing all the facts about Jesus Christ as history without coming to the place of Biblical, that is, personal and saving, faith in Him. Perhaps you are one of these. You need not be; there is yet time and no better time than now to be sure you have eternal life and are on your way to Heaven. "Behold, now is the accepted time; behold, now is the day of salvation" (2 Cor. 6:2b).

Let me ask you through this printed page, Do you really know that you will be secure in Christ for all of eternity? Or do you really wonder, even fear that you may be lost, although you may push the concern from your mind because it is unpleasant to contemplate? It need not be. Jesus Christ loves you more than you can imagine. He died for your sins because He loves you. The cord of His love for you drew Him from Heaven's glory to the cruel cross of Calvary. He shed His blood for your sins. "In whom [Jesus Christ] we have redemption through his blood, the forgiveness of sins, according to the riches of his grace" (Eph. 1:7).

As the Lamb of God, He took away your sins, being a perfect and acceptable sacrifice and substitute for you. What love He has for you. You need not fear death; you need not be in miserable bondage to sin and its transitory and shallow pleasures; you need not be punished by the holy God. Like His only begotten Son, He loves you. He gave His only begotten Son for you, expressly that you might be forgiven, repenting of your sin and trusting His great love for you in Jesus Christ. You can trust His Word. He has said, "Whosoever shall call upon the name of the Lord shall be saved" (Rom. 10:13). "Him that cometh to me I will in no wise cast out" (John 6:37).

The work for your salvation and mine is already done. "All we like sheep have gone astray; we have turned every one to his own way, and the Lord hath laid on him the iniquity of us all" (Isa. 53:6). The proof that His sacrifice was acceptable payment for our sin before the holy God of love is that Jesus Christ was raised from the dead. "Who was delivered for our offences, and was raised again for our justification" (Rom. 4:25). This means we, and especially you, are saved right now if you believe God's Word to you, and trust Jesus to do what He promised He would; namely, save you if you ask Him to do so. ". . . Ask, and ye shall receive . . ." (John 16:24). "Call unto me, and *I will* answer thee, and show thee great and mighty things, which thou knowest not" (Jer. 33:3).

Friend, Jesus is waiting, just waiting to save you. He came "to seek and to save that which was lost" (Luke 19:10). Believe and call upon Him. He died for you because He loves you. He was raised from the dead that you may be raised to eternal life with Him. Trust Him, call upon Him, He will keep His promise and save you. "For whosoever [that's you] shall call upon the name of the Lord [Jesus Christ] shall be saved [right now, the moment of calling]."

Ask Jesus Christ to save you now. He will.

Appendix A

The Episcopal Church in
The Diocese of Ohio
The Office of the Bishop
January 22, 1971

The Rev. George Rich
37425 Eagle Road
Willoughby Hills, Ohio 44094

Dear George:

I appreciate your sending along to me a copy of your letter of resignation so that I now have the official version of the manner in which you are taking leave of St. Bartholomew's.

You know, I trust, what deep pain of heart this decision of yours gives me. Not only are Martha and I deeply devoted to both Francoise and you as friends, but I have been personally so appreciative of your pastoral concern for people and for your leadership.

Naturally, I believe you have embraced a distortion of what constitutes the proper doctrine and practice of the Church. You appear to be giving yourself to what is in my view a narrow and sectarian view of Christian faith. But we have been over all of that in our discussions and I certainly honor your sincerity and your right of conscience. Our difference in the sacramental meaning of baptism and the effective meaning of salvation will not impair, I trust, our respect and love for one another.

Because you have stated to me personally in my office on Tuesday, January 12 and have reiterated in your letter to St. Bartholomew's Church dated January 17 that you are at odds with the Christian Faith as understood by the Book of Common Prayer, I believe I have no alternative but to suspend you in your exercise of the priesthood until such time as you assure me in writing that you can embrace again the Declaration you took at ordination time in Article VIII of the Constitution. This suspension is undertaken through authority granted me under Article IX and Canon 64.

Needless to say, it would make me very happy to lift this sentence soon after you have wrestled further with the theological and personal problems involved in your understanding of Faith in Jesus Christ.

Please give Francoise my love and know that you are both in my prayers.

Ever sincerely yours,

The Bishop

cc: President of the Standing Committee
    Registrar of the Diocese

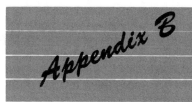

Appendix B

A Sermon
FROM ST. PAUL'S EPISCOPAL CHURCH
AKRON, OHIO

In a recent newsletter it was suggested that sermon topics of special interest be called to the attention of the clergy. One suggestion was that a sermon be preached on the subject, "how to be saved." Although all of the suggestions were interesting, this one especially mobilized my thinking. Therefore it is to a consideration of this concern that this morning's sermon is addressed.

Presumably when one asks that a sermon be preached on "how to be saved" the real and underlying concern is how he or she might be saved. In other words, the question is, "How do I obtain eternal life?" Or again, "How do I secure eternal bliss instead of eternal damnation?" Such questions are certainly valid. As Dietrich Bonhoeffer, a great Christian martyr of this century, once wrote, "There is only one question of paramount importance in the Christian life, and that is, how shall we survive the last judgment." Still, I wonder if man can know the answer to this question, at least in this life. Certainly it could be said that in a sense we are all saved, if by that one meant that the death of Jesus Christ is an accomplished fact, and further that this historical event allows us the possibility of eternal life.

Nevertheless, the fact of His offer of salvation must become real in each person's life if it is to have meaning. And even if one does know the Christ at depth, he still does not know how he will survive the last judgment. He does not know "how to be saved." As Bonhoeffer says, this is the great question of the Christian's life.

The purpose of this sermon therefore will not be to answer the question as to the how of salvation, but rather to help clarify our thinking about the subject generally—at least hopefully.

Let me begin by pointing out that Holy Scripture contains two conflicting attitudes which relate to our consideration of salvation. Because some have seen fit to make absolute one view and thereby rule out the other, misconceptions have arisen. To expose these—and they are both common and dangerous—let us examine the two conflicting trends in the Bible.

The first theme can be discovered in those passages which constantly warn us of God's dreadful judgment. Such passages caution us to always do right, for wrong actions carry with them eternal and abiding consequences. Matthew 5:21 provides a good illustration:

> You have heard that it was said to the men of old, "You shall not kill; and whoever kills shall be liable to judgment." But I say to you that every one who is angry with his brother shall be liable to judgment; whoever insults his brother shall be liable to the council, and whoever says, "You fool!" shall be liable to the hell of fire [RSV].

This Biblical attitude as you see causes our thinking about salvation to move in a moralistic and judgmental way. Such passages suggest that right action is a necessary prerequisite to salvation.

The other conflicting Biblical theme that relates to salvation indicates that it is God's will and purpose that all men should be saved and have eternal life. Thus in 1 Timothy, chapter 2, we read: *"This is good, and it is acceptable in the sight of God our Savior, who desires all men to be saved and to come to the knowledge of the truth"* [RSV]. Or later, in chapter 4, *"For to this end we toil and strive, because we have our hope set on the living God, who is the Savior of all men, especially of those who believe"* [RSV]. In opposition to the other trend, this view places no apparent moral requirement upon the attainment of salvation. This type of thinking which is called universalism, intimates that those who are bad in this life will get another chance in the next one. It maintains that all men must be saved—a comfortable position.

At this point, let us look at the potential dangers of these two Biblical attitudes when they become hardened and exclusive. To think of one's own salvation only in terms of right choice—the first trend—is to ignore or take lightly man's sinfulness. No man is good enough to deserve salvation, and this is true of the best, most holy saints. If man could earn his eternal reward, why would there be any need of Christ? Indeed, historically Protestant Christianity has failed to do justice to man's need of salvation through Christ, rather it has exalted man's own merits. Further, to press for perfection in order to obtain salvation is to invite the sensitive soul to experience unnecessary despair.

On the other hand, to maintain that all men will be saved regardless of their conduct—the second trend—is to deny man's moral concern. Man is created for good and must participate in the mad struggle to be whole. Further, this compulsory salvation denies man's greatest gift of freedom. It might also be pointed out that this view denies God's righteousness, while the first attitude denies His compassion.

Another danger which can result from making absolute only one part of Holy Scripture is that of idolatry. Excessive concern for doing good works can be an attempt to avoid a living confrontation with God. If we can believe that good works will secure our salvation, it is easy to place them before the true God. It is possible to substitute right action for God, in our minds.

Chances are that the good works we choose to do will require less self-giving than the demands that a living confrontation with God would require.

On the other hand, if one is convinced that salvation is his regardless of how he acts, he is likely to put his own will before God's. This is idolatry. The grave peril of idolatry in any form—be it that of good works for selfish reasons or that of pure self-indulgence—is habit. We can become so accustomed to doing what we want that we find it more difficult to do what God wants. Often the fear is expressed—consciously or unconsciously—that God will condemn a soul to hell. Indeed, as indicated, there seems to be a basis for this thinking. Still, the far greater danger may well be that man condemns himself to hell. This quote from the book, *Doctrine in the Church of England,* is revealing.

> As the essence of Hell is exclusion from the fellowship of God, so the essence of Heaven is that fellowship. It is not a selfish happiness offered in reward for self-suppression at an earlier time, it is fellowship with God who is Love. Inasmuch as this is fellowship of the creature with the Creator, of the finite with the Infinite, its characteristic is not Adoration. This is infinite bliss to the soul which is purged of self-interest; to the self-centered soul the experience of that fellowship is not possible at all; but if it were possible, it would not be enjoyable. To put it crudely, if a selfish man could go to Heaven, he would be miserable there.

Before leaving this discussion, it should be noted that the conflicting attitudes in the Bible in no way discredit its authenticity. It merely represents the attempt of men—and men were the authors of the Bible—to proclaim at once God's love and righteousness, His righteousness and His forgiveness. An error is committed only when one side is taken to the exclusion of the other, and then pushed to an extreme. Having said this, let me suggest that there is another, more positive way to think about our question of salvation: namely within the context of a living relationship to God. Instead of using the future as our frame of reference, which is usually done as just indicated, we can center ourselves in the present, in the immediate. We can deal with the certain rather than the uncertain, hopefully avoiding many of the previous pitfalls.

This approach begins by entering into a direct relationship with God, by letting His presence be felt in our lives. Not in some great, dramatic way with thunder claps and booming voices, but in a quiet way—like when we feel His subtle push which causes us to make this decision or take that action. We may wonder if it is really God at work, but when we obey His promptings we discover that He has guided us once more.

Yet, at the same time, we do not like to be dependent; we do not like to obey God. We want to run our own lives, even when we make a mess of things.

In other words, we are always at the crossroads. Each decision we make demands that we do His or our will. As we make our decisions we soon discover that we are moving steadily towards God or away from Him. A general direction is taken.

As we move more fully into God's presence we feel both joy and sorrow. Joy in that we know Him more fully, sorrow in that we become more aware of our unworthiness. We become aware of our unfaithfulness when compared to His unerring integrity. At this point we are aware of our own need of forgiveness. We become deeply aware of our need of the Lord; we become aware of our need for salvation.

In other words, as we live our lives within the framework of Christian growth—which I have very briefly and simply tried to portray—our thinking about salvation becomes part of our total being. Salvation is not thought of in terms of how to be saved, or in terms of future abstractions which are uncertain. Rather we think of salvation in terms of a living, growing relationship between Father and child. The child knows that he deserves to be severely punished. He can only repent and hope his Father will be merciful. He can only hope that his faith in the

Mediator, Whom the Father has sent, will bring the promised victory. But with this hope—within the life of faith—is to be found sure confidence—and that peace which passes all understanding.

THE REVEREND GEORGE E. RICH, JR.
SIXTEENTH SUNDAY after TRINITY
SEPTEMBER 13, 1964

Notes

Chapter one

1. The Episcopal church consists of two orders, clergy and laity. The order of clergy consists of bishop, priest and deacon. The bishop has authority over the churches in his territory or diocese. Priests and deacons serve in various capacities in the dioceses but usually in a parish or mission church. A rector is a priest in charge of a parish (local church) and a vicar is a priest in charge of a mission church (a church that is not self-supporting). Deacons are usually seminary graduates on the way to ordination to the priesthood. The office of deacon is usually a short-term office, more or less a trial period. These deacons are called curates if they are assistants on a church staff.

Chapter two

1. An acolyte is a boy (usually) who assists the priest during services. Some would refer to an acolyte as an altar boy.

2. Sensitivity Training, in my opinion, can be a devastating experience to certain personality types. It is basically negative, even destructive, because it removes people's defenses without giving any resource with which to replace them. Hence, much promiscuity resulted from these conferences as hurt people tried to comfort one another. Although church-sponsored, there was no Biblical or genuine spiritual resource. Christ was

not preached. It was totally humanistic. Fortunately, God's grace again saved me from excesses at such conferences.

3. All of the counseling that I knew about in the church at this time was based on the premise that self-acceptance, even of sin, will finally give one the freedom to change the undesirable behavior, i.e., undesirable because the individual wants it changed. God's Word or other absolute standards were not in the picture.

Chapter four

1. Copies of the letter were sent to the president of the standing committee and the registrar of the diocese.

2. For instance, the House of Bishops did not defrock Bishop James Pike, who denied the virgin birth and the deity of Christ.

Chapter five

1. The Episcopal church takes pride in drawing wide lines regarding doctrine. It allows a great deal of latitude in belief. The Thirty-nine Articles of Religion of the Church of England is the most official statement of doctrine, though many church members know it only by name.